My Christian Year

Cath Senker

HODDER
Wayland

an imprint of Hodder Children's Books

Titles in this series

My Buddhist Year • My Christian Year • My Hindu Year
My Jewish Year • My Muslim Year • My Sikh Year

Conceived and produced for Hodder Wayland by

Nutshell
MEDIA

Intergen House, 65-67 Western Road, Hove BN3 2JQ, UK
www.nutshellmedialtd.co.uk

Editor: Polly Goodman
Inside designer and illustrator: Peta Morey
Cover designer: Tim Mayer
Consultant: Jane Clements, The Council of Christians & Jews

Published in Great Britain in 2002 by Hodder Wayland, an imprint of Hodder Children's Books.

British Library Cataloguing in Publication Data
Senker, Cath
My Christian year. - (A year of religious festivals)
1. Fasts and feasts - Juvenile literature
2. Church year - Juvenile literature
I. Title
394.2'66

ISBN 0 7502 4062 8

Printed in Hong Kong by Wing King Tong.

Hodder Children's Books
A division of Hodder Headline Limited
338 Euston Road, London NW1 3BH

Acknowledgements: The author would like to thank Janay, June and Colin Bromley, and Morgan O'Flaherty, Head of St Mary Magdalen School, Brighton, for all their help in the preparation of this book.

Picture Acknowledgements:
Art Directors and Trip Photo Library 4 (B. Turner), 8, 22, 23 (H. Rogers); Britstock Cover (Tsuyoshi Kishimoto), 10 (Hinata Haga), 12 (Hideo Haga), 14 (Tsuyoshi Kishimoto), 21 (Takashi Yoshida); Circa Photo Library 16, 25 (John Frye), 26, 27; Eye Ubiquitous Title page, 9, 11 (Bennett Dean), 18 (Mike Kipling), 19 (L. Fordyce), 24 (Mike Alkins); Hodder Wayland Picture Library 7 (Penny Davies), 15 (Zak Waters), 17 (Stuart Weir); Impact 20 (Christophe Bluntzer); Nutshell Media 5 (Yiorgos Nikiteas), 13 (Sue Cunningham); World Religions 6 (Christine Osborne).

Cover photograph: Dressed up for carnival in Trinidad and Tobago.
Title page: A harvest festival procession in Barbados.

Contents

A Christian life

Christians believe there is one God. He made the world and looks after it. God loves every living creature.

Christians believe that Jesus is the Son of God. They follow Jesus' teachings in their holy book, the Bible. Christians feel that God's power is always with them. It is called the Holy Spirit.

Christians worship in churches. This girl has lit some candles in a church in Greece.

This is Janay. She has written a diary about the Christian festivals.

Janay's diary
Wednesday 12 November

My name's Janay Bromley. I'm 9 years old. I've got a brother called Mitchell and a sister, Ciara. We have a hamster called Pumpkin. I love swimming and going shopping. At home I like reading and playing with my sister and my friends. We're members of the Catholic Church.

There are many Christian festivals. Most festivals celebrate events in Jesus' life, especially his birth and death.

The Christian symbol is the cross.

Sundays

Every Sunday

Sunday is the Christian holy day. It is a day of rest. People like to spend the day with their family and church friends.

At church, the priest or minister gives a sermon. He or she reads from the Bible. People pray and sing hymns or other songs.

These Christians are singing and dancing in church to worship God.

Many children go to Sunday school to learn about being a Christian.

Some Christians worship quietly. Others prefer loud, joyful church services.

Janay's diary
Sunday 23 November

We went to church this morning. Our church is run by Father Foley. He is nice and he always helps people. Today I was an altar girl. I like being part of the church community. On Sundays we read the Bible. We always have a family lunch. I like Sundays because I get to spend lots of time with my family.

Advent

30 November–24 December

Advent is the start of the Christian year. Christians prepare for Christmas by thinking about how they could become better people.

Advent calendars and candles help to count down the days until Christmas Day.

This girl is lighting the first candle on an Advent ring.

Janay's diary
Monday 8 December

Today was the ninth day of Advent. I opened another door of my Advent calendar. I'm really excited about Christmas - only 16 more days to go! Yesterday at church the priest lit the second Advent candle. He wore a special robe and talked about the birth of Jesus. At school today we rehearsed for the school play. I'm going to sing carols with the choir, too.

One door on an Advent calendar is opened every day until Christmas.

Some churches have an Advent ring. It has four coloured candles and one big white candle. On the first Sunday of Advent, one coloured candle is lit. Every Sunday one more is lit until all four are alight. The white candle is lit on Christmas Day.

Christmas

24 December–6 January

At Christmas, Christians celebrate the birth of Jesus. No one knows exactly when Jesus was born.

Most people celebrate Christmas on 25 December. Orthodox Churches hold the festival on 6 January. Many churches hold a service on Christmas Eve. It is called Midnight Mass.

A Christmas parade in Perth, Australia. In Australia, Christmas falls in the summer. Many people celebrate outdoors.

A nativity scene in Goa, India. Christians believe that Jesus was born in a stable in Bethlehem.

Christmas Day is a holiday in many countries. People go to church and sing carols. At home they give presents and have a special meal.

Janay's diary
Thursday 25 December

Last night, on Christmas Eve, we read the Christmas story. We hung up our stockings and said our prayers. This morning we woke up early – it's Christmas Day and I was too excited to sleep! We gave our baby Jesus doll a kiss and put him in his toy crib. Then we opened our presents. After Mass we had Christmas lunch. I always think of Jesus on Christmas Day. Without him we would not have Christmas.

Epiphany

6 January

Epiphany celebrates the story of the Wise Men. They came to see baby Jesus, bringing three special gifts.

Epiphany means 'to make known' in Greek. Christians are happy that Jesus was made known to many people.

Children dressed up as the Wise Men, in Austria. The Wise Men brought gifts of gold, frankincense and myrrh.

Spanish children in a procession to celebrate the Wise Men's visit to baby Jesus.

But the king was not happy. He thought that Jesus might try to take his throne. So he told his soldiers to kill all Jewish baby boys. Luckily, Jesus escaped with his parents, Mary and Joseph.

Janay's diary
Tuesday 6 January

Today it was Epiphany. We went to Mass with Nanny and Grandad, Auntie Jackie and my cousins. Some of the children from the church acted out the story of the Wise Men. The Wise Men followed a special star, which led them to baby Jesus. The story shows how important Jesus was because the Wise Men travelled for a long time to find him.

Shrove Tuesday

February

Shrove Tuesday is the day before Lent. Some Christians go to confession. They tell their priest about any bad things they have done and pray to God to forgive them.

Young dancers at a Lent carnival in Trinidad and Tobago.

This boy is making pancakes on Shrove Tuesday.

In Britain, Shrove Tuesday is Pancake Day. In the USA and France it is Mardi Gras (which means Fat Tuesday). People make pancakes. In the past, this was to use up fatty foods before Lent. In some countries, there is a carnival.

Janay's diary

Wednesday 25 February

Yesterday it was Shrove Tuesday. Daddy made pancakes from flour, eggs and milk. We ate them with lemon juice – they were yummy! We decided what to give up for Lent. My whole family gave up something. I decided to give up sweets. Giving up something for Lent helps us to be thankful for what we have every day.

Lent

March/April

Lent lasts for 40 days before Easter. Christians think about things they have done wrong. They believe that if they are sorry, God will forgive them.

On Ash Wednesday, at the start of Lent, ash is put on people's foreheads to say sorry for anything they have done wrong.

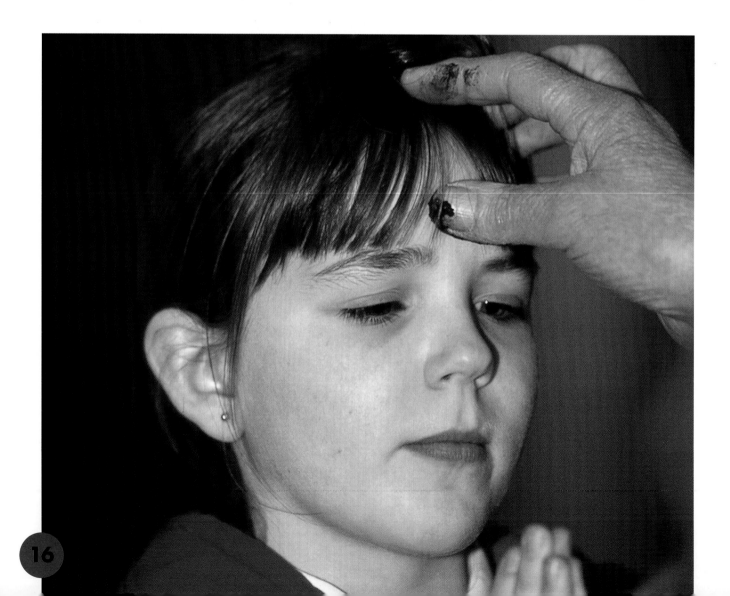

At Lent, Christians try to give up a food they enjoy, such as sweets. It reminds them that Jesus spent 40 days in the desert without food.

Mothering Sunday is during Lent. People say prayers for their mothers and give them a present.

This girl has given her mother some flowers for Mothering Sunday.

Janay's diary
Sunday 28 March

Today it was Mother's Day. We made breakfast in bed for Mum to show how much we love her. Then we went to church. Afterwards we took Mum out for lunch. I haven't eaten any sweets for over a month because it's Lent. There are still another 13 days to go. It's been really hard giving up sweets but it's worth it. Mum says it's good for my teeth, too.

Holy Week

March/April

The last week of Lent is Holy Week. It is the most important Christian festival. People celebrate the last week of Jesus' life.

On Palm Sunday they remember how Jesus rode into Jerusalem on a donkey. Many churches hold processions and people carry crosses made out of palm leaves.

A Palm Sunday procession in Spain, with a statue of Jesus.

Christians around the world remember Jesus dying on the cross. This ceremony is in the Philippines.

On Maundy Thursday, Christians think about the Last Supper that Jesus had with his friends. Then on Good Friday, they remember how Jesus died on the cross.

Janay's diary
Friday 9 April

Today it was Good Friday. We bought hot cross buns for tea and ate them hot with melted butter – delicious! The buns have crosses on the top to remind us that Jesus died on the cross. This week at school we learnt all about how Jesus died. We heard how his friends were very sad. It was a very busy week at school learning about things.

Easter Sunday

March/April

On Easter Sunday, Christians remember Jesus' Resurrection. It is a joyful day.

After dying on the cross, Jesus rose from the dead. This was a wonderful miracle. It showed that life could win over death.

On Easter Sunday, churches are decorated with spring flowers. The church bells ring out.

People light candles and lamps. The candles and lamps stand for new life.

These Greek Christians are at Mass on the night before Easter Sunday.

An Easter parade in the USA. Some people wear colourful eggs.

Janay's diary
Sunday 11 April

Today was Easter Sunday. I wanted to open my Easter eggs but we had to wait until after church. It was nice to celebrate Jesus rising from the dead because he is so special. Easter eggs stand for new life. We give them to remember how Jesus was given new life after he died. When we got back from church we gave Easter eggs to each other and had a big family meal.

Ascension and Pentecost

May/June

Forty days after Easter, Christians celebrate Ascension Day. They believe that 40 days after his Resurrection, Jesus ascended (rose) to heaven to be with God.

Ten days after Ascension Day is Pentecost. Christians remember the coming of the Holy Spirit. This is God's power working in the world.

A banner showing the coming of the Holy Spirit upon Jesus' followers.

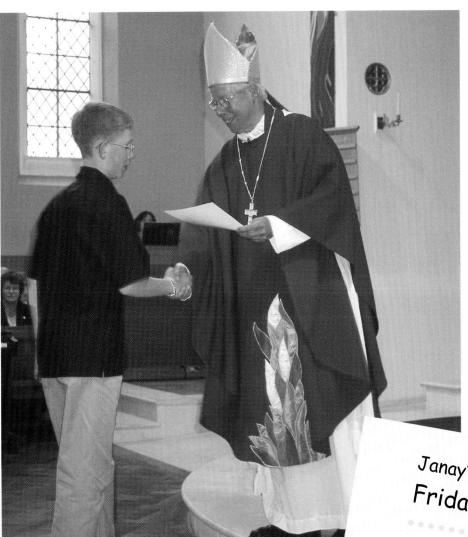

At Pentecost, new members are welcomed to the Christian Church. This boy is at a special ceremony called confirmation.

The Holy Spirit helped Jesus' followers to spread his teachings. This was the beginning of the Christian Church. Pentecost is the Church's birthday.

Janay's diary
Friday 21 May

Yesterday it was Ascension Day. At school we learnt about Jesus' ascension to heaven. It was very important because it helped people to believe what Jesus taught. We thought about Jesus going up to heaven. Then we had to paint what we thought it was like. I drew a big flash of light rising up to the sky.

Harvest festival

September/October

Harvest festival is in the autumn.
It celebrates all the foods and
flowers that grow in the earth.

Christians thank God for these good
things. They decorate their church
with fruit, vegetables and flowers.

**A harvest festival
procession in
Barbados.**

These children have brought bread and corn dollies to church for the harvest festival.

Janay's diary
Wednesday 22 September

Today it was harvest festival. We brought lots of food into school for people who needed it. There was a harvest display at Mass. We gave thanks to God for giving us rain and sun to help the harvest. The priest talked a lot about the needy. Afterwards, I went with the Brownies to the old people's home. We brought food and helped to make tea.

Christians like to share food with people who are not as lucky as they are. Often they take presents of food to people in need. They collect goods to send to people in poor countries.

All Saints' Day

1 November

On All Saints' Day, Christians remember all their saints. Saints are people who lived a good life. They followed Christian ways and helped other people.

Some saints were killed because they were Christians. For their good deeds, the Church made them saints.

Some saints have their own day, when people remember them. On All Saints' Day, Christians honour the saints who don't have their own special day. People sing hymns about them in church.

A picture of Saint George, the saint who protects England. His saint's day is 23 April.

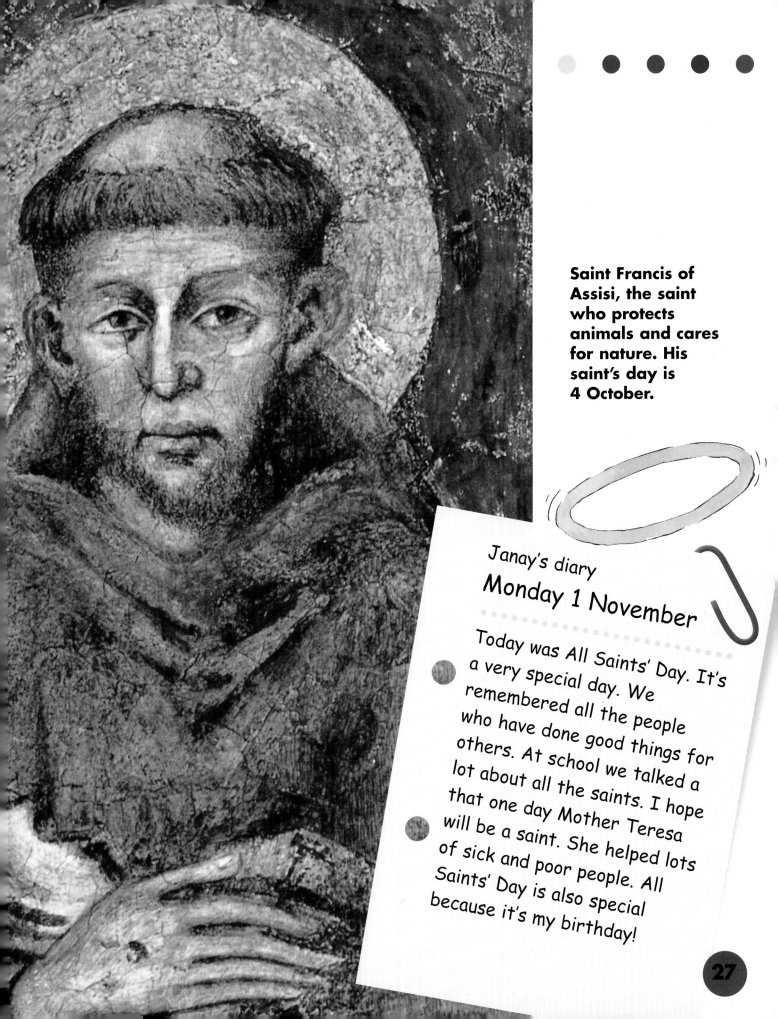

Saint Francis of Assisi, the saint who protects animals and cares for nature. His saint's day is 4 October.

Janay's diary

Monday 1 November

Today was All Saints' Day. It's a very special day. We remembered all the people who have done good things for others. At school we talked a lot about all the saints. I hope that one day Mother Teresa will be a saint. She helped lots of sick and poor people. All Saints' Day is also special because it's my birthday!

Christian calendar

30 November–24 December

Advent

Christians prepare for Christmas.

24 December–6 January

Christmas

People celebrate the birth of Jesus.

6 January

Epiphany

This festival celebrates the Wise Men visiting baby Jesus.

February

Shrove Tuesday

The last day before Lent.

February/March/April

Lent

Christians remember the forty days that Jesus spent in the desert without food.

Ash Wednesday

The shape of a cross is marked on people's foreheads with ash.

March/April

Holy Week

Christians remember the last week of Jesus' life.

Easter Sunday

People remember Jesus rising from the dead.

May/June

Ascension Day

People remember the day that Jesus rose up to heaven.

Pentecost

This is the birthday of the Church.

September/October (in northern hemisphere)

Harvest festival

People thank God for giving us food from the earth.

1 November

All Saints' Day

Christians celebrate their saints.

Glossary

Advent A time of preparation for four weeks before Christmas. 'Advent' means 'coming'.

altar girl (or boy) A child who helps the priest in church.

Bible The Christian holy book.

carnival A big festival, with music and dancing in the streets.

Catholic Church The Roman Catholic Church is led by the Pope, or Holy Father.

Church The whole community of Christians. A church is also a building where Christians meet.

community The people who live in the local area. Here it means the Christians living in the area.

confession Telling the priest about any bad things you have done.

Father Another name for priest.

holy Connected with God.

Holy Spirit The power of God in the world today. The Holy Spirit helps people to do what God wants.

honour To show that you admire and respect someone.

hymns Religious songs that Christians sing together in church.

Last Supper The last meal that Jesus ate with his followers.

Lent The season of forty days before Easter.

mass A service that uses bread and wine to help people remember Jesus.

minister In some churches, the minister is the person in charge.

Mothering Sunday Also called Mother's Day. It is celebrated on the fourth Sunday of Lent in Britain and on the second Sunday in May in the USA.

nativity The birth of Jesus Christ.

Orthodox Churches Churches such as the Russian and Greek Church. They are sometimes called the Eastern Churches.

palm A straight tree with no branches and lots of long leaves at the top.

priest The person in charge of a Catholic church.

Resurrection Jesus' rising from the dead.

sermon A talk about a religious topic.

services Religious ceremonies in church.

Notes for teachers

pp4–5 Christians believe Jesus is God in human form. God is a Holy Trinity, with three parts: Father (God), Son (Jesus) and the Holy Spirit. The Holy Spirit is the presence of God in Christians' lives today. The Bible is made up of the Old Testament (the Jewish Bible) and the New Testament (about Jesus' life and the early Church).

pp6–7 Sunday is the Christian day of rest and worship. Churches often hold two services, one in the morning and one in the evening. Services vary greatly. Many Christians attend Holy Communion, a service using the symbols of bread and wine to remember Jesus. In some churches, such as the Methodist and Baptist Churches, the sermon is the main feature of the service. Various churches use music and drama to make their services lively. Children often attend Sunday school, where they learn about Christianity.

pp8–9 Christians believe that stories in the Old Testament foretold the coming of Jesus, so during Advent, readings in church focus on these Bible stories. Christians also believe that Jesus will 'come again' to earth, this time in power and glory, which is particularly remembered at Advent. They prepare for the coming of Christ by thinking about how they can be better people. Some Christians have an Advent candle at home, numbered from 1 at the top down to 24 at the bottom, to represent the days of Advent. On each day in December the candle is lit until it burns down to the next number. It lasts until Christmas Day.

pp10–11 Christmas is the second most important Christian festival after Easter. Janay hangs up her stocking for Father Christmas to fill it with presents. Father Christmas has different names in different countries. In the USA, children call him Santa Claus; in Austria and the Czech Republic he is Saint Nicholas. Many churches hold Midnight Mass so that people can feel close to Jesus on the night when they remember his birth. Most Christians attend church on Christmas Day, where they thank God for bringing them Jesus and give money to the Christmas collection.

pp12–13 The Church is made up of the Catholic, Protestant and Orthodox traditions. The Orthodox Church, including the Russian and Greek Churches, celebrates Christmas on 6 January, the day when Jesus was shown to the Wise Men of the East, or 'Three Kings' as they are called in popular tradition. The gifts they brought were symbols: gold was for a king (Christians call Jesus the King of Kings); frankincense was used in worship, and myrrh was a perfume put on dead bodies, and Jesus was to die. At Epiphany, Christians hold a special Mass.

pp14–15 Christians used to confess their sins so they could make a fresh start and feel pure for Lent. On Shrove Tuesday, people had to remove all rich foods from the house so they would not be tempted to eat them during the Lent fast. Traditionally a feast was held; today pancakes are usually made. The word 'carnival' comes from the Latin words meaning 'farewell to meat'. In some countries, such as Brazil, big processions with decorated floats parade through the streets. Great merriment precedes the seriousness of Lent.

pp16–17 Ash Wednesday is the first day of Lent. The ash cross, made from the ashes of burnt palm crosses, is a sign of penitence. In early Church times, only one small meal a day, not containing animal products, was eaten during Lent. Nowadays, most Christians observe Lent by giving up something they enjoy. In some countries Mothering Sunday is during Lent. In the past, this was the day when young women servants were allowed home to visit their mothers. Many Christians undertake charitable activities during Lent.

pp18–19 The Palm Sunday procession commemorates Jesus' ride into Jerusalem on a path strewn with palm leaves. Everyone holds a cross made from a palm leaf. On Maundy Thursday, Christians recall Jesus' last meal with his disciples. He washed their feet to teach them humility. Today, some priests wash people's feet; in Britain, the Queen gives money to pensioners. On Good Friday, the most solemn day of the year, Christians remember Jesus' crucifixion by the Roman rulers of Jerusalem, who saw him as a threat to Roman authority.

pp20–21 Christians believe Jesus died on the cross to atone for people's sins. They believe that he was resurrected, and that his spirit lives on to inspire them today. The theme of Easter is the victory of light over darkness, of life over death. In Catholic churches, everyone lights their own candle from the Paschal candle, and the church fills with light. Many Easter customs involve painted eggs, hard-boiled eggs or chocolate eggs; the eggs are a symbol of new life.

pp22–3 On Ascension Day, always a Thursday, there are special prayers in church. Pentecost celebrates the miraculous event when Jesus' disciples experienced the power of the Holy Spirit within them. It gave them the courage to go out into the world on a mission to carry on Jesus' work. Pentecost is therefore the birthday of the Church. Christians believe God's spirit lives on in all those who follow Jesus. Traditionally, Pentecost is a time for admitting new members to the Church through baptism.

pp24–5 Harvest festival celebrates God's role in nature. It takes place in September or October in the northern hemisphere, and between March and May in the southern hemisphere. In Britain, produce is brought into the church and blessed; people also pray for a good harvest in the following year. Special hymns are sung, thanking God for providing food from the earth. Harvest is a time for sharing, so many churches collect food or other basic necessities to distribute to those in need.

pp26–7 The early saints were people who were close to Jesus, and Christians who were martyred under the Roman Empire. Over the years, many people who have been seen as especially holy have been named as saints, and given their own saint's day. Roman Catholic and Orthodox Christians ask the saints to pray for them. They believe these prayers will have special power. Protestant Christians generally don't agree with the idea of praying to saints; they feel people should pray directly to Jesus.

Other resources

Artefacts

Articles of Faith, Resource House, Kay Street, Bury BL9 6BU. Tel. 0161 763 6232

Religion in Evidence, 28b Nunnbrook Road Industrial Estate, Huthwaite, Notts NG17 2HU Tel. 0800 318686

Books to read

Celebrate: Christmas by Mike Hirst (Hodder Wayland, 1999)
Celebrate: Easter by Mike Hirst (Hodder Wayland, 2000)
Celebrate: Harvest by Polly Goodman (Hodder Wayland, 2000)
Christian Festival Tales by Saviour Pirotta (Hodder Wayland, 2000)
Christian Festivals Cookbook by Saviour Pirotta (Hodder Wayland, 2000)
I am a Roman Catholic by P. Pettenuzzo (Franklin Watts, 2001)
Looking at Christianity: Festivals by Graham Owen and Alison Seaman (Hodder Wayland, 1998)
Looking at Christianity: Special Occasions by Kathleen Miller (Hodder Wayland, 1999)
Places of Worship: Catholic Churches by Clare Richards (Heinemann, 2000)
Places of Worship: Orthodox Churches by Geoff Robson (Heinemann, 2000)
Places of Worship: Protestant Churches by Mandy Ross (Heinemann, 1999)
What do we know about: Christianity? by Carol Watson (Hodder Wayland, 2001)

Photopacks

Christians photopack, by the Westhill Project, available from Adrian Leech, Westhill RE Centre, Tel. 0121 415 2258. E-mail: a.leech@bham.ac.uk
Living Religions: Christianity posterpacks 1 and 2, with booklets, from Thomas Nelson and Sons.

Websites

www.cafod.org.uk/schools/ CAFOD's website
www.canterbury-cathedral.org
www.cofe.anglican.org The Church of England website
www.dwtcg.kent.sch.uk/relinks.htm Has links to all religions
www.theresite.org.uk Includes curriculum resources and IT in RE pages with details of CD-Roms, software and videos, and TV and radio programmes.
www.underfives.co.uk/events.html Lists the dates of main festivals for all major religions.

Index